2010~2011
COLLEGE BASKETBALL GUIDE

★ ★

BY JIM GIGLIOTTI

Beach Ball Books

Produced by Shoreline Publishing Group LLC
Santa Barbara, California
Editorial Director: James Buckley, Jr.
Designer: Tom Carling, www.carlingdesign.com
Research: Matt Marini

Photo Credits
Cover:
Left to right: Purdue's JaJuan Johnson (Robbins Photography), Baylor's Brittney Griner (AP/Wide World), Duke's Kyle Singler (AP/Wide World), and Michigan State's Durrell Summers (Robbins Photography). Back Cover: Left: Tennessee's Angie Bjorklund (AP/Wide World). Right: Purdue's Robbie Hummel (Robbins Photography).
Interior:
AP/Wide World: 3 (bottom), 4 (2), 5, 6, 7 (2), 8, 11, 12, 16, 17, 18, 19 (2), 21 (top), 22 (bottom), 23 (2), 24 (top), 27 (top), 28, 29, 30 (2), 31 (3), 32 (top left, bottom left), 33 (right), 34 (3), 35 (right), 36 (bottom), 37 (2), 38 (2), 39 (2), 40 (2), 41 (2), 42, 43 (2), 44 (2), 45, 47. Robbins Photography: 3 (top), 9, 10, 13, 14, 15, 20 (2), 21 (bottom), 22 (top), 24 (bottom), 25 (2), 26 (2), 27 (bottom), 32 (right), 33 (left), 35 (left), 36 (top).

ISBN 13: 978-1-936310-01-2
ISBN 10: 1-936310-01-5

10 9 8 7 6 5 4 3 2 1   09 10 11 12 13

Printed in the U. S. A.
First printing, October 2010

CONTENTS

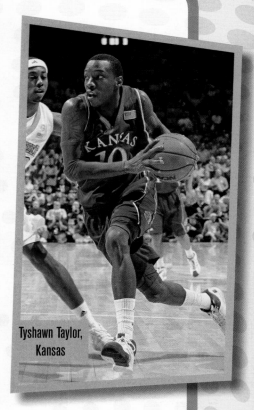

Tyshawn Taylor, Kansas

Angie Bjorklund, Tennessee

A Season to Remember

IN THE END, Goliath beat David. The Big Boys beat the Little Guys. It wasn't supposed to be that way. The storybook finish would have had the underdog beating the favorite on a last-second shot. Instead, that shot bounced off the rim, and the Duke University Blue Devils of the mighty Atlantic Coast Conference held on to beat the Butler Bulldogs of the lesser-known Horizon League 61–59 in the championship game of the NCAA Men's Basketball Tournament in Indianapolis, Indiana, last April.

A great game capped a great season that college basketball fans will long remember. It featured inspired individual play from stars such as Kentucky's **John Wall** and Ohio State's **Evan Turner**.

Wall, a point guard, was one of four freshman starters for the Wildcats. He was named the Southeastern Conference Player of the Year after averaging 16.6 points, 4.3 rebounds, and 6.5 assists per game. In June, he became the top overall pick of the NBA Draft (by the Washington Wizards).

Turner, who played guard and forward, broke two bones in his back in December. But he returned to the line-up after missing only six games. He went on to average 20.4 points, 9.2 rebounds, and 6.0 assists and earn the Wooden Award and Naismith Trophy as college basketball's best player.

Neither Wall nor Turner could take their teams to a title, though. The NCAA Tournament was filled with upsets, last-second game-winning shots, and a range of emotions from thrilling victories to agonizing defeats.

Kansas entered the postseason as the tournament favorite. The Jayhawks looked good in a first-round win, but then were stunned by Northern Iowa in the second round.

With the victory, Northern Iowa made it to the Sweet 16. The ninth-seeded Panthers weren't even one of the most surprising teams of the tournament, though: eight teams seeded No. 10 or lower pulled off upsets in the opening round. Talk about your bracket busters!

There was no more surprising team than Butler. The Bulldogs were seeded fifth, but had to survive a gauntlet of great teams such as Syracuse, Kansas

Gordon Hayward, Butler

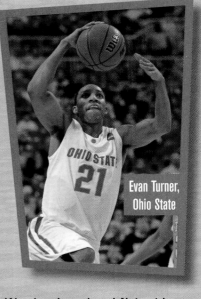

Evan Turner, Ohio State

Tipoff at the 2010 championship game

State, and Michigan State to make it to the final.

Duke, meanwhile, didn't have the star power that some of its other great squads have had. But the Blue Devils came together as a team and really hit their stride in February, when they began a streak that carried them to 18 wins in their last 19 games.

The championship game was close all the way, with Duke finally opening a 60–55 lead in the final minutes. Butler pulled within one point and had a chance to take the lead, but **Gordon Hayward** missed a short jumper in the closing seconds. With 3.6 seconds left, the Blue Devils made one free throw but missed the second. Hayward got the rebound, dribbled to halfcourt, and let fly the final shot. The ball

bounced off the backboard and then the front rim. Just missed! Duke had its fourth national title.

It was fitting that the championship was in doubt all the way to the final buzzer because all season long it was anybody's guess what team would end up as champion.

Kansas entered the season as the favorite and got off to a terrific start. But after the Jayhawks stumbled, Texas rose to the top of the polls. That didn't last long, though, and soon it was Kentucky's turn. Then Kansas was back on top. Syracuse was No. 1 for a bit, too. Ironically, Duke never made it to the top during the regular season—but the Blue Devils did when it counted the most!

MEN'S PREVIEW

Tipoff to 2010-2011

THE BIGGEST NEWS in men's college basketball this season is that the National Collegiate Athletic Association (NCAA) has decided to expand its tournament from 65 teams to 68 teams. (See the "First Four" box on page 8.) That means even more of the upsets, last-second game-winning shots, thrilling victories, and agonizing defeats that happen in "March Madness."

Expanding the field opens up a lot of questions for 2010-11. Will the extra three spots go to so-called "mid-major" schools (teams that don't play in the biggest conferences)? Or will they just mean more spots for the "Big Six" conferences that already get the most teams in? Will it be more difficult for a Cinderella team such as Butler last year to make it all the way to the final game? Or will more teams make it harder for the Dukes and the Michigan States to avoid an upset?

Fans of the expanded tournament argue that more is better. Opponents say, "If it ain't broke, don't fix it!" These kinds of preseason debates are what makes sports fun! We argue, and then we get to see who is right by the results on the field...er, court.

There's a lot more to the college basketball season than just March Madness, though. There are several months' worth of exciting games leading up to the NCAA Tournament.

This year, especially, it will take that long to get to know all the star players and teams. Most of the big names from last season either graduated or left for the NBA. It figures to be a wide-open chase for the championship.

But what can we guess this season will bring? Well, turn to page 9 to see our picks for the best teams of 2010-11. Then keep reading to find out how the conference races shape up (page 25) and what players figure to be the biggest stars of this season (page 30). And don't forget about women's hoops. Turn to page 42 for a preview of the women's game. (Hint: Connecticut is No. 1...again.)

It's time for tipoff!

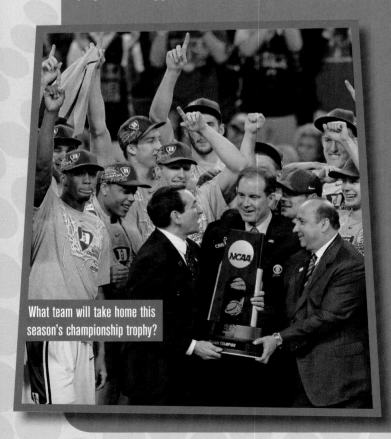

What team will take home this season's championship trophy?

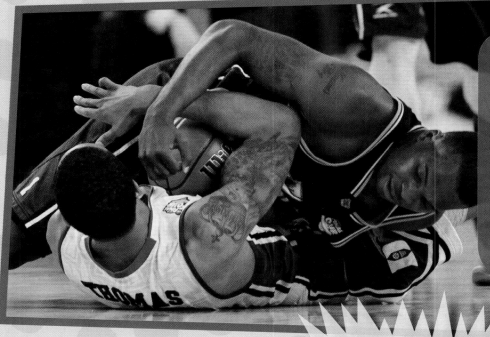

Duke vs. Butler: The Rematch

The Butler Bulldogs get another chance to topple the Duke Blue Devils when the teams meet in a rematch of the 2010 NCAA title game. Duke beat Butler 61–59 in that one, when the Bulldogs' long, last-second shot bounced off the rim. The rematch is scheduled for December 4 at the Izod Center in East Rutherford, New Jersey.

Circle This Date!

March 13, 2011 is Selection Sunday. That's the day to find out if your team made it into the NCAA Tournament—or, if you already know that your team has qualified, to find out where and when it will be playing.

Midnight Madness

Nearly 40 years ago, Maryland's men's basketball team began the tradition of "Midnight Madness." (Now the school calls it "Maryland Madness.") The Terrapins started at the stroke of midnight on the first day that NCAA rules allowed for practice, and they turned it into a party for the fans. This season, October 15 was the first official day of practice. But now, NCAA rules allow the first practice to start at a more reasonable time!

First Four

We know how big the Final Four has gotten. But this season, there's something new: the First Four. That's First Four, as in the first four games of the NCAA Tournament (as opposed to the Final Four, which is the last four teams alive in the tourney).

In the offseason, the NCAA decided to expand the tournament from last season's 65 teams (which was whittled to 64 after one "play-in" game). Officials considered 80 teams, or even 96. In the end, they decided on 68 teams. The four lowest rated teams (No. 65 through 68) will play in two of the First Four games. The last four "at-large" teams (teams that did not win their conference but were invited to the Tournament anyway) will play in the other two First Four games.

By playing the First Four, the NCAA Tournament field is reduced from 68 teams to a tidy 64 teams entering the second round (because 64 easily moves down to 32 teams after the next round of games, and then to 16 teams, and then to 8, 4, and 2 until only 1 champion remains).

The reality, though, is that the First Four is only a, well, first step until the NCAA Tournament expands even more, perhaps to 96 teams one season in the near future.

Reliant Stadium

Other Important Dates

Tuesday, March 15, 2011
The first "First Four" is schedule to begin in Dayton, Ohio.

Thursday, March 17, 2011
Second-round games in the NCAA Tournament begin at various sites around the country. By the end of the day on Sunday, March 20, the tourney will be down to the "Sweet 16."

Thursday, March 24, 2011
The regional round of the NCAA Tournament begins. The Final Four will be set by the end of the action on Sunday, March 27.

April 2, 2011
The Final Four begins at Reliant Stadium in Houston, the home of the NFL's Houston Texans.

April 4, 2011
The championship game of the NCAA Tournament will be played at Reliant Stadium.

TOP 20

HERE ARE OUR PICKS FOR THE TOP 20 men's teams for the 2010-11 season. (Let the arguments begin!) Your team may or may not be ranked for now. But, as Duke and Butler proved last year, it's not where you begin the season that matters—it's where you end it.

NO.1 Purdue

Choosing the Boilermakers as the best team in the nation is as easy as one-two-three.

That's one, as in one Big Ten title in 2009-10; two, as in two consecutive trips to the NCAA Tournament's Sweet 16; and three, as in three of the best returning players in the nation.

Last season's regular-season conference championship (shared with Michigan State and Ohio State) was Purdue's first in 14 years, and the Boilermakers didn't lose in the NCAA Tournament until running into eventual-national-champion Duke in the third round. But the Boilermakers were left to wonder what might have been after sharp-shooting forward **Robbie Hummel** injured his knee late in the regular season and missed the Big Ten and NCAA Tournaments.

Hummel is expected to be back healthy this year, and he joins fellow returning starters **E'Twaun Moore**, a guard, and **JaJuan Johnson**, a center. They were the Boilermakers' top three scorers and rebounders last year.

E'Twaun Moore

COACH **Matt Painter**

CONFERENCE **Big Ten**

2009-10 RECORD **29–6 (14–4)**

POINTS! **E'Twaun Moore, G (16.4)**

BOARDS! **JaJuan Johnson, C (7.1)**

IN THE *PAINT*

The Boilermakers are the only team among the "Big Six" conference schools to return three first-team all-league players from 2009-10.

LEGEND: Record in parentheses = conference mark; Points! = Leading returning scorer (and points per game in parentheses); Boards! = Leading returning rebounder (and rebounds per game in parentheses).

IN THE PAINT

The Blue Devils, who are seeking their second consecutive national title, have done it before: They won back-to-back championships in the 1990–91 and 1991–92 seasons.

COACH Mike Krzyzewski
CONFERENCE Atlantic Coast
2009-10 RECORD 35–5 (13–3)
POINTS! Kyle Singler, F (17.7)
BOARDS! Kyle Singler, F (7.0)

Nolan Smith

NO.2 Duke

Even head coach **Mike Krzyzewski** probably would admit that the Blue Devils arrived one year ahead of schedule when they won the national championship last season. It was this year, with an experienced group of returning players, that Duke and its fans expected a run at the national title.

Okay, maybe Duke and its fans expect a run at the national title every year. But the point is, with so many seasoned and talented players returning from last year's 35–5 champs, the Blue Devils have every reason to believe they can win again this year. In fact, Duke likely will be ranked No. 1 in most preseason polls.

Guard **Jon Scheyer**, the leading scorer from last year, is off to the NBA, but forward **Kyle Singler** and guard **Nolan Smith** are key returnees. They'll be joined by guard **Kyrie Irving**, one of the top incoming freshmen in the nation.

Jamar Samuels

NO.3 Kansas State

The Wildcats like to wear down teams with an aggressive, up-tempo style so they need a lot of team depth—and the good news is that this year's team is loaded with players back from last year's squad. Nine lettermen return from a team that reached the Elite Eight of the NCAA Tournament last season.

The most important of the returnees is guard **Jacob Pullen**, who made 110 three-pointers and averaged 19.3 points per game last season. The third-team All-America selection thought about turning pro, but decided to come back for his senior year.

Another key senior is forward **Curtis Kelly**, a transfer from Connecticut who made a big impact in his first year with Kansas State last year. Forward **Jamar Samuels** was the Big 12's Sixth Man of the Year for 2009-10.

COACH **Frank Martin**

CONFERENCE **Big 12**

2009-10 RECORD **29–8 (11–5)**

POINTS! **Jacob Pullen, G (19.3)**

BOARDS! **Curtis Kelly, F (6.2)**

COACH **Billy Donovan**
CONFERENCE **Southeastern**
2009-10 RECORD **21–13 (9–7)**
POINTS! **Kenny Boynton, G (14.0)**
BOARDS! **Alex Tyus, F (6.9)**

NO.4 Florida

It was only a few seasons ago that Florida was the top team in college basketball. The Gators won the national championship in 2005-06. Then they won it all again in 2006-07 to become the first repeat champions since Duke in the early 1990s. Florida didn't exactly disappear after that, but the Gators haven't won an NCAA Tournament game since. (In the past three years, they've been to the NIT twice and the NCAAs once.) This year, that should change.

Head coach **Billy Donovan** has his best squad since those title-winning teams. The Gators return all five starters from a team that won 21 games before a tough, double-overtime loss to BYU in the opening round of the NCAA Tournament. All five of those starters averaged in double figures, including guards **Kenny Boynton** and **Erving Walker**.

The Gators have a balanced group that plays together well—a lot like those NCAA championship teams a few years back.

Kenny Boynton

IN THE PAINT

In the summer, incoming freshman center **Patric Young** played for the Under-18 U.S. National Team that won the gold medal at the FIBA Americas U18 Championship.

NO.5 Villanova

The Wildcats were a pretty good team in 2009-10, when they won 25 games and advanced to the second round of the NCAA Tournament. But this year, they might even be better.

For Villanova to improve, though, someone will have to step up in place of guard **Scottie Reynolds**. He was one of the best players in the nation last season, but he was a senior and is trying to make it in the NBA now. A combination of several guards likely will pick up the slack, including emerging stars **Maalik Wayns** and **Dominic Cheek**, who were freshmen last season.

Mouphtaou Yarou and **Maurice Sutton** give Villanova lots of size up front. A long list of talented returnees also includes guards **Corey Fisher** and **Corey Stokes** and forward **Antonio Pena**.

IN THE PAINT

Villanova won 20 of its first 21 games in 2009-10 before a late-season slump. They were ranked as high as No. 2 in the nation.

Corey Fisher

COACH **Jay Wright**
CONFERENCE **Big East**
2009-10 RECORD **25–8 (13–5)**
POINTS! **Corey Fisher, G (13.3)**
BOARDS! **Antonio Pena, F (7.0)**

COACH **Tom Izzo**
CONFERENCE **Big Ten**
2009-10 RECORD **28—9 (14—4)**
POINTS! **Kalin Lucas, G (14.8)**
BOARDS! **Draymond Green, F (7.7)**

NO.6 Michigan State

The biggest offseason news in East Lansing (the home of the Spartans) is that head coach **Tom Izzo** turned down a chance to coach the NBA's Cleveland Cavaliers and decided to stay at Michigan State.

Not only that, but after annually being rumored as a candidate to coach in the pros, Izzo announced that he was staying at the school "for life." That's great news for Spartans' fans because under his watch, the school has become a national powerhouse in basketball.

Last season, Michigan State made it to the NCAA Tournament's semifinal game before dropping a two-point decision to Butler. This season, the Spartans will try for a return trip to the Final Four behind senior guards **Kalin Lucas** and **Durrell Summers**.

One big loss is forward **Raymar Morgan**, who was a senior last season—but that's not as big a loss as Izzo would have been.

IN THE PAINT
The Spartans have made it to the Final Four six times since the 1998-99 season. That's more than any other school in the country in that span.

Durrell Summers

NO.7 Ohio State

In June, former Ohio State star **Evan Turner**, last season's college player of the year, was selected by the Philadelphia 76ers with the No. 2 pick of the NBA Draft. You might think that with such a superstar gone, Ohio State figures to be in for some tough times—but think again!

The Buckeyes made it to the Sweet 16 last season, and even without Turner this year, they are still loaded with talent. Guard **William Buford** was second on the team only to Turner in both scoring and rebounding in 2009-10, and **Jon Diebler** is a sharp-shooting guard who drained 116 three-pointers last season. Swingman **David Lighty** is another key returnee.

Add in perhaps the best group of freshmen in the country, plus a rugged schedule that will be good preparation for the NCAA Tournament, and the Buckeyes figure to be in the national-title hunt again this season.

IN THE PAINT

What is a "buckeye"? It comes from the buckeye tree and is a shiny, dark-brown nut with a light tan patch. Carrying one around is supposed to bring good luck.

William Buford

COACH **Thad Matta**

CONFERENCE **Big Ten**

2009-10 RECORD **14−4 (29−8)**

POINTS! **William Buford, G (14.4)**

BOARDS! **William Buford, G (5.6)**

COACH **Mark Few**
CONFERENCE **West Coast**
2009-10 RECORD **27–7 (12–2)**
POINTS! **Elias Harris, F (14.9)**
BOARDS! **Elias Harris, F (7.1)**

IN THE PAINT

The Zags (as the Bulldogs sometimes are called) have won the West Coast Conference's regular-season championship 10 years in a row.

NO. 8 Gonzaga

It is a tribute to head coach **Mark Few** and the program that he has built in the Pacific Northwest that Gonzaga was disappointed with a second-round loss in the NCAA Tournament last year. Yes, expectations are so high now that 27 victories even in what was supposed to be a rebuilding year are not enough.

It was a rebuilding year because the Bulldogs had lost four starters from the season before. This year, there is no such starting over, as the team lost only one starter from last season. That player was a good one: guard **Matt Bouldin**, who was the conference player of the year. But a candidate for this year's conference player of the year is one of the key returnees. It's forward **Elias Harris**, who averaged 14.9 points and a team-leading 7.1 rebounds per game as a freshman in 2009-10. Harris probably will be a first-round draft pick in the NBA one day.

Ashton Gibbs

AUTO PARTS

NO.9 Pittsburgh

Just like No. 8 Gonzaga, Pittsburgh was in rebuilding mode in 2009-10 after losing four starters from the previous season… and just like Gonzaga, the Panthers made it all the way to the second round of the NCAA Tournament, anyway.

That means even higher expectations for 2010-11, when a deep and experienced roster returns. An excellent backcourt, led by guards **Ashton Gibbs** and **Brad Wanamaker**, is the biggest strength. But the Panthers have size, depth, and experience up front, too. **Gary McGhee**, a 6-10 center, finally asserted himself as a junior last season. Now the Panthers hope that **Dante Taylor** does the same this year. A much-ballyhooed incoming freshman last season, Taylor didn't live up the hype, but could make a bigger impact this year.

COACH **Jamie Dixon**
CONFERENCE **Big East**
2009-10 RECORD **25−9 (13−5)**
POINTS! **Ashton Gibbs, G (15.7)**
BOARDS! **Gary McGhee, C (6.8)**

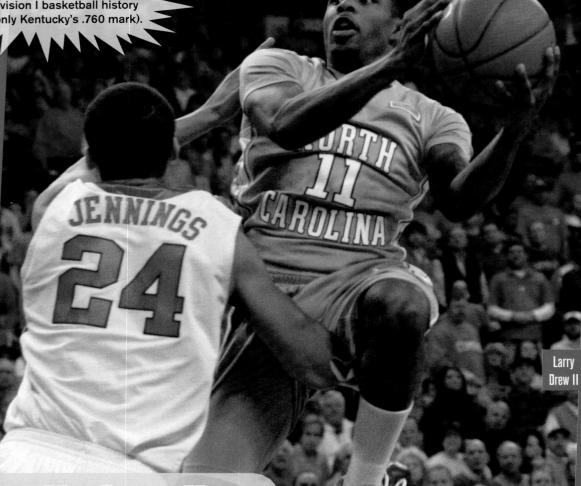

IN THE PAINT

North Carolina's all-time winning percentage of .736 ranks second in NCAA Division I basketball history (behind only Kentucky's .760 mark).

Larry Drew II

NO. 10 North Carolina

What happened to North Carolina last year? The Tar Heels, who are almost always really good, won their fifth national championship in the 2008-09 season, but then did not even make it to the NCAA Tournament in 2009-10. Still, 20 wins and a trip to the NIT title game isn't exactly a disaster, even if it's not up to the school's usual lofty standards.

The general feeling is that the Tar Heels have way too much talent to fall short of the NCAA Tournament again this year. Several players from last year's team are gone, but the list of highly regarded returnees includes point guard **Larry Drew II** and forward **John Henson**. They'll be joined by a great group of freshman highlighted by **Harrison Barnes**, the No. 1 recruit in the country.

Barnes, who can play either guard or forward, already is being projected by some draftniks as the No. 1 overall pick in next season's NBA Draft. But first things first: He'll help North Carolina back into the national picture in 2010-11.

COACH **Roy Williams**
CONFERENCE **Atlantic Coast**
2009-10 RECORD **20−17 (5−11)**
POINTS! **Will Graves, G/F (9.8)**
BOARDS! **Will Graves, G/F (4.6)**

NO. 11 Butler

The Bulldogs pretty much snuck up on everyone in their run to the NCAA title game last season. But now their cover is blown, and everyone knows how good they can be.

Gordon Hayward, who launched the final shot against Duke, is gone to the NBA. Star guard **Shelvin Mack**, though, leads a team that is the best in the Horizon League again. Expect to see the Bulldogs back in the NCAA Tournament in March.

COACH **Brad Stevens**

CONFERENCE **Horizon League**

2009-10 RECORD **33–5 (18–0)**

POINTS! **Shelvin Mack, G (14.1)**

BOARDS! **Matt Howard, F (5.2)**

IN THE *PAINT* Butler was the only NCAA Division I team to win every conference game it played in 2009-10.

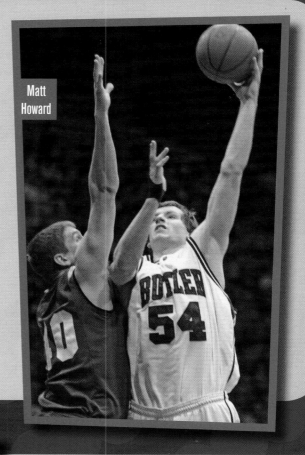

Matt Howard

Quincy Acy

NO. 12 Baylor

This year's Final Four will be at Reliant Stadium in Houston, Texas. That's only about a three-hour drive from the Baylor campus, and the Bears are dreaming of playing for the national championship so close to home after making it to the Elite Eight last season.

To get there, Baylor will need a big season from senior shooting guard **LaceDarius Dunn** and junior forward **Quincy Acy**. Those returning stars figure to get help from center **Perry Jones**, who is one of the best incoming freshmen in the nation.

COACH **Scott Drew**

CONFERENCE **Big 12**

2009-10 RECORD **28–8 (11–5)**

POINTS! **LaceDarius Dunn, G (19.6)**

BOARDS! **Quincy Acy, F (5.1)**

IN THE *PAINT* The Bears' first-round victory over Sam Houston State last year marked its first win in the NCAA Tournament in 60 years.

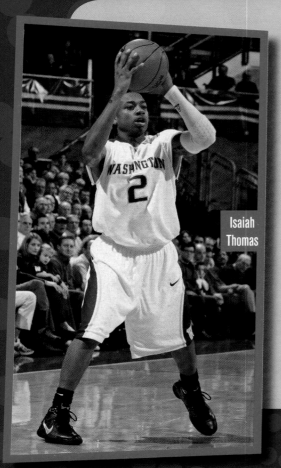

Isaiah Thomas

NO. 13 Washington

The Huskies were one of only two Pac-10 teams to make the NCAA Tournament last season. After making it to the Sweet 16, they can probably count on another trip to the Big Dance this year. Almost the whole team is back—well, except for forward **Quincy Pondexter**, who was the team's leading scorer.

Losing Pondexter, who was a senior, hurts. But **Isaiah Thomas** might be the best guard in the Pac-10, and center **Matthew Bryan-Amaning** gives Washington a big man up front. **Abdul Gaddy** is expected to emerge as a key man at point guard in his sophomore season.

COACH **Lorenzo Romar**

CONFERENCE **Pac-10**

2009-10 RECORD **26–10 (11–7)**

POINTS! **Isaiah Thomas, G (16.9)**

BOARDS! **Matthew Bryan-Amaning, F (5.9)**

IN THE PAINT Washington reached the Sweet 16 of the NCAA Tournament for the third time in the last six seasons in 2010.

NO. 14 Kansas

The Jayhawks have some work to do after losing several of the players that helped them earn the top overall seed in the NCAA Tournament last year. (They were upset in the second round by Northern Iowa.) But Kansas is one of those schools that just always seems to be good. As the old saying goes, they don't rebuild—they reload.

Twins **Marcus** and **Markieff Morris** give the Jayhawks a couple of key big men inside, while freshman guard **Josh Selby** is expected to make an immediate impact outside.

COACH **Bill Self**

CONFERENCE **Big 12**

2009-10 RECORD **33–3 (15–1)**

POINTS! **Marcus Morris, F (12.8)**

BOARDS! **Marcus Morris, F (6.1)**

IN THE PAINT The Jayhawks have won the Big 12's regular-season championship six years in a row.

Marcus Morris

NO. 15 Syracuse

Kris Joseph

The Orangemen have to replace some really good players who have graduated or gone on to the NBA, including **Wesley Johnson**, the 2009-10 Big East Player of the Year. But **Jim Boeheim** is another one of those coaches who always seems to have more stars coming in to take over for those who left.

This season's top players figure to be guard **Scoop Jardine** and forward **Kris Joseph**. But the biggest star—at least physically—is incoming center **Fab Melo**, a 7-footer who is expected to play a key role right away.

COACH Jim Boeheim

CONFERENCE Big East

2009-10 RECORD 30–5 (15–3)

POINTS! Kris Joseph, F (10.8)

BOARDS! Rick Jackson, F (7.0)

IN THE PAINT Kris Joseph was the Big East Sixth Man of the Year for 2009-10, while **Scoop Jardine** earned the national Sixth Man award.

NO. 16 Kentucky

No school was hit harder this year by the recent trend of "one and done"—one season of college basketball, then on to the NBA—than Kentucky. The Wildcats started four freshmen last season, but all of them turned pro after the NCAA Tournament.

Now, coach **John Calipari** has another great recruiting class on its way. The biggest names to know are guard **Brandon Knight**, forward **Terrence Jones**, and center **Enes Kanter**. It will be tough to win relying on freshmen, but the Wildcats won 35 games doing it last year.

COACH John Calipari

CONFERENCE Southeastern

2009-10 RECORD 35–3 (14–2)

POINTS! Darius Miller, G (6.5)

BOARDS! Darnell Dodson, G (2.5)

IN THE PAINT The Wildcats have won more games and played in the NCAA Tournament more times than any other school in history.

John Calipari

NO. 17 Illinois

The Fighting Illini are in just about the opposite situation of No. 16 Kentucky: Every one of Illinois' key players are back. A couple, such as guard **Demetri McCamey** and forward **Mike Davis**, decided to return for their senior seasons instead of turning pro.

That's the good news for head coach **Bruce Weber** and the Illini fans. The bad news is that even with such standout players, Illinois still lost 15 games in 2009-10 and missed the NCAA Tournament. They should be back in the Big Dance this year, though.

COACH **Bruce Weber**

CONFERENCE **Big Ten**

2009-10 RECORD **21–15 (10–8)**

POINTS! **Demetri McCamey, G (15.1)**

BOARDS! **Mike Davis, F (9.2)**

IN THE *PAINT* At 7.1 assists per game, guard **Demetri McCamey** ranked No. 2 in the nation in the 2009-10 season.

Demetri McCamey

Kawhi Leonard

NO. 18 San Diego State

San Diego State has never won an NCAA Tournament game (in six tries), but this could be the year that changes. Head coach **Steve Fisher** quietly has built a formidable team that won the Mountain West Conference tournament last season and is ready to be a factor on the national scene this year.

All the key players from last season's 25-win team are back for the Aztecs, including forward **Kawhi Leonard**. He led the team in scoring and rebounding as a freshman last year.

COACH **Steve Fisher**

CONFERENCE **Mountain West**

2009-10 RECORD **25–9 (11-5)**

POINTS! **Kawhi Leonard, F (12.7)**

BOARDS! **Kawhi Leonard, F (9.9)**

IN THE *PAINT* The Aztecs have played in a postseason tournament a school-record five seasons in a row.

NO. 19 Missouri

Missouri bills itself as the "Fastest 40 Minutes in Basketball." Head coach **Mike Anderson's** team features an attacking defense that (in theory, at least) creates turnovers and leads to easy baskets on the offensive end. It's non-stop intensity.

To make that work, Anderson needs a lot of depth. And even though the Tigers lost three key seniors from last year's team, a talented recruiting class fills the void, while junior guards **Kim English** and **Marcus Denmon** provide the veteran leadership.

COACH **Mike Anderson**

CONFERENCE **Big 12**

2009-10 RECORD **23−11 (10−6)**

POINTS! **Kim English, G (14.0)**

BOARDS! **Laurence Bowers, F (5.7)**

IN THE **PAINT** The Tigers' relentless defense produced a nation-leading 10.9 steals per game in 2009-10.

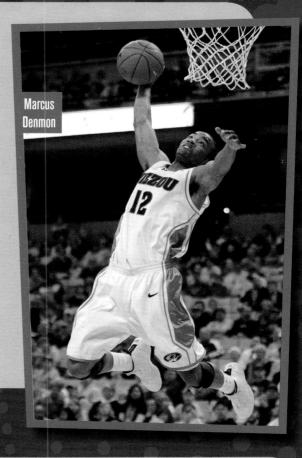

Marcus Denmon

Jackson Emery

NO. 20 BYU

The Cougars' 2009-10 season ended with a second-round loss to Kansas State in the NCAA Tournament, but by then they already had won a school-record 30 games.

They'll try to improve on that this year behind star guard **Jimmer Fredette**, a third-team All-America choice in 2009-10. Fredette instantly makes the Cougars formidable, but he has plenty of help, too. **Jackson Emery**, his teammate in the backcourt, gives BYU one of the best guard tandems in the country. Like Fredette, Emery was an All-Mountain West Conference pick last season.

COACH **Dave Rose**

CONFERENCE **Mountain West**

2009-10 RECORD **30−6 (13−3)**

POINTS! **Jimmer Fredette, G (22.1)**

BOARDS! **Noah Hartsock, F (5.1)**

IN THE **PAINT** The Cougars have won at least 25 games four seasons in a row.

Five More To Watch

GEORGIA

The Bulldogs will go as far as dynamic forward Trey Thompkins can take them.

COACH **Mark Fox**

CONFERENCE **Southeastern**

2009-10 RECORD **14–17 (5–11)**

POINTS! **Trey Thompkins, F (17.7)**

BOARDS! **Trey Thompkins, F (8.3)**

MEMPHIS

If the players in a great recruiting class can jell, the Tigers could be really good.

COACH **Josh Pastner**

CONFERENCE **Conference USA**

2009-10 RECORD **24–10 (13–3)**

POINTS! **Wesley Witherspoon, F/G (12.5)**

BOARDS! **Will Coleman, F (6.2)**

Will Coleman, Memphis

Rick Majerus, St. Louis

ST. LOUIS

The Billikens won 23 games last year and appear ready to make a big step up.

COACH **Rick Majerus**

CONFERENCE **Atlantic 10**

2009-10 RECORD **23–13 (11–5)**

POINTS! **Kwamain Mitchell, G (15.9)**

BOARDS! **Willie Reed, F (7.9)**

UNLV

Head coach Lon Kruger has this once-formidable program on the rise again.

COACH **Lon Kruger**

CONFERENCE **Mountain West**

2009-10 RECORD **25–9 (11–5)**

POINTS! **Tre'Von Willis, G (17.2)**

BOARDS! **Chace Stanback, F (5.8)**

VIRGINIA TECH

The Hokies have a chip on their shoulder after being overlooked on Selection Sunday last year.

COACH **Seth Greenberg**

CONFERENCE **Atlantic Coast**

2009-10 RECORD **25–9 (10–6)**

POINTS! **Malcolm Delaney, G (20.2)**

BOARDS! **Jeff Allen, F (7.4)**

CONFERENCE PREVIEWS

THE TOP 20 TEAMS are sure to get most of the attention this season. But there are a whole lot of other spots up for grabs in the 68-team NCAA Tournament this year. Let's take a quick look at schools around the country. We'll start with the "Big Six" conferences—the ACC, Big 12, Big East, Big Ten, Pac-10, and SEC—and then make our way to the rest of the leagues in NCAA Division I men's basketball. Plus, check out the notes and news for many teams.

2010 STANDINGS

1. *Duke* ②
   Maryland
3. *Florida State*
   Virginia Tech
5. *Wake Forest*
   Clemson
7. *Georgia Tech*
8. *Boston College*
9. *Virginia*
   North Carolina ⑩
   North Carolina State
12. *Miami*

ACC

Top to bottom, the Atlantic Coast Conference can claim to be the best college basketball league in the nation. The ACC is the only conference to have each of its teams play in the NCAA Tournament at least once in the last five seasons, and its five national championships in the 2000s equal the total of all other conferences combined.

➤ **Boston College:** **Steve Donahue** is the new head coach for the Eagles. He has four starters returning from last year's 15–16 team, including top scorer **Joe Trapani.**

➤ **Florida State:** Forward **Chris Singleton** is the best defender on a great defensive team: The Seminoles held opponents to a nation-low 37.7 shooting percentage in 2009-10.

➤ **Maryland:** Head coach **Gary Williams** will try to lead the Terrapins to their 18th consecutive postseason berth, but he has to do it with only two starters back from last year's team.

Chris Singleton
Florida State

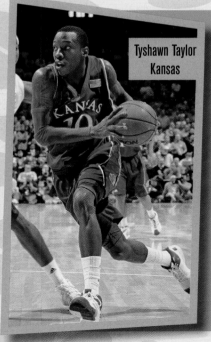

Tyshawn Taylor
Kansas

2010 STANDINGS

1. *Kansas* ⑭
2. *Kansas State* ③
   Baylor ⑫
   Texas A & M
5. *Missouri* ⑲
6. *Texas*
   Oklahoma State
8. *Colorado*
9. *Texas Tech*
   Iowa State
   Oklahoma
12. *Nebraska*

BIG 12

The Big 12 soon will have a different look because Colorado is heading to the Pac-10 after this coming season, and Nebraska will be joining the Big Ten. For this season, though, you can expect more of the same from last season, when a league-record seven teams earned NCAA Tournament bids.

➤ **Colorado:** The Buffaloes will rely on a pair of stellar guards in **Alec Burks**, who set a school record for points by a freshman last year, and **Cory Higgins**.

➤ **Texas:** The Longhorns are aiming for their 12th consecutive season of 20 or more wins and their 13th year in a row in the NCAA Tournament.

➤ **Texas A & M:** The Aggies' 69–53 victory over Utah State in the 2010 NCAA Tournament marked the fifth season in a row that they won an opening-round game.

➤ **Texas Tech:** Point guard **John Roberson** already is the Red Raiders' career assists leader heading into his senior season.

Boldface: 2010 Conference tournament winner.   Orange circle: Ranking on our Top 20 List.   *Italic:* played in 2010 NCAA Tournament.

2010 STANDINGS

1. *Syracuse* 15
2. *Pittsburgh* 9
   West Virginia
   Villanova 5
5. *Marquette*
   Louisville
7. *Notre Dame*
   Georgetown
9. South Florida
   Seton Hall
11. Cincinnati
    Connecticut
13. St. John's
14. Rutgers
15. Providence
16. DePaul

BIG EAST

When they call it the Big East, they really mean "big"! That's big as in 16 teams, and big as in big-time play, too. There are a lot of really good teams in this league. Half of the Big East teams made it into the NCAA Tournament last year . . . and could again this year.

➤ **Connecticut:** Point guard **Kemba Walker** is the man who makes the offense go. But he'll need a lot of help to get the Huskies back to their accustomed heights.

➤ **Notre Dame:** The Irish made the NCAA Tournament last season but they have to replace forward **Luke Harangody**, who led the Big East in scoring. He was drafted by the NBA's Boston Celtics.

➤ **St. John's:** **Steve Lavin** is the Storm's new coach. Lavin last coached at UCLA, where he took the Bruins to the NCAA Tournament six consecutive seasons from 1996-97 to 2001-02.

➤ **West Virginia:** The Mountaineers made it to the Final Four last season, but the going will be tougher this year with forwards **De'Sean Butler** and **Devin Ebanks** in the NBA now.

Kemba Walker
Connecticut

John Leuer
Wisconsin

2010 STANDINGS

1. *Purdue* 1
   Ohio State 7
   Michigan State 6
4. *Wisconsin*
5. *Illinois* 17
6. *Minnesota*
7. Northwestern
   Michigan
9. Indiana
   Iowa
11. Penn State

BIG TEN

This figures to be the toughest conference in the nation in 2010-11. Purdue, Michigan State, Ohio State, and Illinois expect to be among the nation's best. But Minnesota, Northwestern, and Wisconsin aren't all that far behind, either.

➤ **Indiana:** It's hard to believe that the Hoosiers lost 21 games last year. But head coach Tom Crean is rebuilding around a solid corps of players, including guards **Maurice Creek** and **Verdell Jones III**.

➤ **Minnesota:** The Golden Gophers, who made a great run to the title game of the Big Ten Tournament last year, feature 6-11 **Ralph Sampson III** and 6-10 **Colton Iverson** up front.

➤ **Northwestern:** The Wildcats have never made it to the NCAA Tournament. But after back-to-back NIT berths, this could be the year.

➤ **Wisconsin:** At 6-10, forward **Jon Leuer** is an All-America candidate who can score from inside or outside.

Boldface: 2010 Conference tournament winner.   Orange circle: Ranking on our Top 20 List.   *Italic:* played in 2010 NCAA Tournament.

2010 STANDINGS

1. *California*
2. Arizona State
3. *Washington* 13
4. Arizona
5. USC
   Oregon State
   UCLA
8. Oregon
   Stanford
10. Washington State

PAC-10

The Pac-10 had a down year last year. Washington and California were the only two schools that earned NCAA Tournament bids. But Arizona and UCLA, two traditionally strong teams, should rebound from the surprisingly poor seasons they had last year.

➤ **Arizona:** The Wildcats' string of 25 consecutive NCAA Tournament berths ended with their 16–15 record last year.

➤ **Oregon State:** Head coach **Craig Robinson's** claim to fame: He's President Obama's brother-in-law.

➤ **Washington State:** The Cougars return all five starters from last year's 16–15 team. Among them: All-Conference guard **Klay Thompson** (19.6 points per game), who is a candidate for All-America honors this season.

Klay Thompson
Washington State

Rotnei Clarke
Arkansas

2010 STANDINGS

EAST

1. *Kentucky* 16
2. *Vanderbilt*
3. *Tennessee*
4. *Florida* 4
5. South Carolina
6. Georgia

WEST

1. Mississippi
   Mississippi State
3. Arkansas
4. Alabama
   Auburn
6. LSU

SEC

The good news for Southeastern Conference fans is that the league always seems to be loaded with individual stars. The bad news is that those players are so talented many of them head to the NBA before they finish college. Incoming freshmen will play a key role in keeping this conference near the top in 2010-11.

➤ **Alabama:** Forward **JaMychal Green** is a great rebounder and shot blocker who will be counted on to help carry the offense this season, too.

➤ **Arkansas: Rotnei Clark** and **Marshawn Powell** are the top returning scorers from a 2009-10 team that showed promise before fading.

➤ **Auburn: Tony Barbee** is the new head coach. The Tigers hope he can turn them around like he did UTEP, which made the NCAA Tournament under his direction last year.

➤ **Tennessee:** The Volunteers reached the Elite Eight for the first time ever last season. It will be difficult for them to get that far again this year, though, as top players **Wayne Chism**, **Bobby Maze**, and **J.P. Prince** were seniors.

More Conferences

AMERICA EAST Forward Tommy Brenton leads 2010 regular-season champ Stony Brook. It was Vermont, though that went to the NCAA Tournament by winning the conference tourney.

ATLANTIC SUN Four teams shared last year's regular-season title, but fifth-place East Tennessee State was the upset winner of the conference tournament.

ATLANTIC 10 Defending NIT-champion Dayton features one of the country's most dynamic players in forward Chris Wright.

BIG SKY Montana was the surprise winner last season, but Weber State is the favorite this year.

Chris Wright
Dayton

BIG SOUTH Coastal Carolina won 28 games last year, but star forward Joseph Harris was a senior. Winthrop annually is the team to beat in the conference tournament.

BIG WEST UC Santa Barbara made the NCAAs last season. Conference Player of the Year Orlando Johnson makes the Gauchos the favorite again.

CONFERENCE USA Tim Floyd is the new head coach at UTEP, the defending champ. Floyd is a former Chicago Bulls' head man, and last coached at USC.

COLONIAL ATHLETIC ASSOCIATION After winning the 2010 College Basketball Invitational, Virginia Commonwealth eyes the NCAA Tournament in 2011.

HORIZON LEAGUE Butler is the team to beat in this conference—no team beat the Bulldogs in league play last season, and few are likely to this year.

IVY LEAGUE Cornell was a surprise Sweet 16 team last year, but Princeton may be the team to beat this year.

METRO-ATLANTIC ATHLETIC Siena's hopes for a fourth consecutive trip to the NCAA Tournament took a hit when coach Fran McCaffrey left to rebuild Iowa.

MID-AMERICAN Ohio had a poor regular season in 2009-10 before winning the conference tournament. Akron and Kent State are the teams to beat, though.

MID-EASTERN ATHLETIC Preseason favorite Morgan State is coached by former California coach Todd Bozeman and led by forward Kevin Thompson, last season's MEAC Defensive Player of the Year.

MISSOURI VALLEY Northern Iowa made a stunning run to the Sweet 16 last season. Missouri State won the Collegeinsider.com Tournament. But Wichita State is the conference favorite this year.

MOUNTAIN WEST This is probably the best conference outside of the "Big Six." BYU, New Mexico, San Diego State, and UNLV all could be repeat NCAA Tournament teams.

NORTHEAST Robert Morris, which nearly upset Villanova in last season's NCAA Tournament, loses a lot of firepower this year. Co-regular-season-champ Quinnipiac is the favorite.

OHIO VALLEY Murray State returns three starters from the team that stunned Vanderbilt in the NCAA Tournament last season and nearly beat Butler in the second round.

PATRIOT Lehigh guard C.J. McCollum was one of the best freshmen in the country last season. He's back as the Mountain Hawks try for a repeat trip to the NCAA Tournament.

SOUTHERN Wofford, which gave a scare to Wisconsin in the NCAA Tournament, returns almost all of the key components from last year's team—the best in school history.

SOUTHLAND Forward Gilberto Clavell is back for his senior season, so Sam Houston State, even with a new coach, is the preseason favorite to win the conference again.

SUMMIT Oakland (Michigan) cruised to last year's conference title and returns one of the top big men in the nation in center Keith Benson.

SUN BELT Among last year's top teams (North Texas, Troy, and Middle Tennessee State), North Texas has the most experienced group of returning players.

SWAC Arkansas Pine-Bluff made the NCAA Tournament last year after starting its season 0–11, but getting back will be an even tougher chore with seven seniors departing for life beyond college.

WAC Utah State seeks its eighth NCAA Tournament bid in 12 years. Forward Tai Wesley leads a deep and experienced roster.

WEST COAST Gonzaga and St. Mary's have dominated this league in recent seasons, but Loyola Marymount is on the rise. The Lions won only three games in 2008-09, but 18 in 2009-10.

Tai Wesley
Utah State

STAR POWER!

COLLEGE BASKETBALL FANS talked a lot in the summer of 2010 about the big names that left to join the NBA Draft even though they still had eligibility remaining—guys like Kentucky's John Wall and Ohio State's Evan Turner. But the college basketball cupboard hasn't been left bare. Here are some of the exciting players you're sure to hear a lot about this season.

GUARDS

Jimmer Fredette,
BRIGHAM YOUNG

When you watch Fredette play, it may not seem like he does anything spectacular. But by game's end, you realize he does just about everything really well. He scored 37 points in a win against Florida in the NCAA Tournament last season.

LaceDarius Dunn,
BAYLOR

Dunn is a shooter, plain and simple. He averaged 19.6 points per game for Baylor last year while taking the majority of his shots from behind the three-point arc. When he's on, he can shoot the lights out.

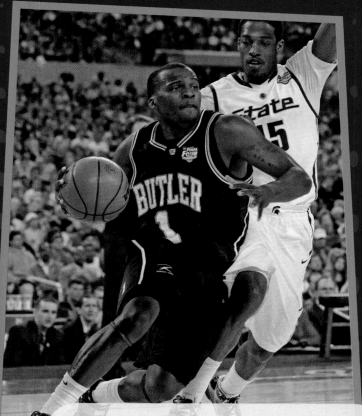

Jacob Pullen, KANSAS STATE

A lot of basketball fans think Kansas State has a team that can reach the Final Four. One reason is because Pullen, who scored 34 points in a win over BYU in last year's NCAA Tournament, came back for his senior season instead of turning pro.

Shelvin Mack, BUTLER

It's tempting to dismiss Butler's incredible run to the championship game last season as a fluke. But that wouldn't be fair to the many talented players on the Bulldogs' team—like Mack, who averaged 14.1 points per game as a sophomore.

Kalin Lucas, MICHIGAN STATE

The Spartans might have played in the NCAA title game for the second year in a row last season if their star point guard didn't hurt his Achilles in a second-round victory. Lucas hopes to help his team make another run at the title in his senior year.

OTHERS:

Malcolm Delaney,
VIRGINIA TECH

Larry Drew II,
NORTH CAROLINA

Isaiah Thomas,
WASHINGTON

Jimmy Butler,
MARQUETTE

Butler was one of the most improved players in the country last season, when he averaged 14.9 points and developed a knack for knocking down game-winning shots. This year, the Golden Eagles are counting on even more from him.

Elias Harris,
GONZAGA

At 6–8 and 215 pounds, Harris is strong enough to muscle his way under the basket, but also is athletic enough to use finesse when needed. He made a big impact as a

Robbie Hummel,
PURDUE

The Boilermakers were heading for a No. 1 seed in the NCAA Tournament last season until Hummel hurt his knee late in the regular season. He's a great shooter whose healthy return helps give his team Final Four hopes this year.

FORWARDS

yle Singler, UKE

e defending national mps are one of the fa-ites to win it all again s year because the ster is still loaded with nt. Singler, a 6–8 ward with the ability to p back and hit threes, at the top of the list.

Trey Thompkins,
GEORGIA

Thompkins can post up and play with his back to the basket or hurt opponents with his jumper. He had a terrific sophomore season in 2009–10 (17.7 points, 8.3 rebounds per game) to earn all-conference honors.

Keith Benson,
OAKLAND

Benson averaged a double-double last season (17.3 points and 10.5 rebounds per game) while leading the Golden Grizzlies to 26 victories and an NCAA Tournament appearance.

MOREHEAD STATE

Even though he's "only" 6–8, Faried is a rebounding machine. His leaping ability and basketball instincts helped him earn Ohio Valley Conference Player of the Year honors for 2009-10.

Player of the Year

College basketball's equivalent of football's Heisman Trophy is actually two trophies! The Wooden Award, named in honor of former UCLA coach John Wooden, and the Naismith Award, named in honor of basketball founder Dr. James Naismith, are each presented annually to the top male and female college players. Ohio State's **Evan Turner** (pictured with the Wooden Award) won both trophies on the men's side last year. This season's finalists won't be announced until December, but here's our take on the leading men's candidates for 2010-11:

1. **Kyle Singler,**
   F, Duke

2. **Elias Harris,**
   F, Gonzaga

3. **Jimmer Fredette,**
   G, Brigham Young

4. **JaJuan Johnson,**
   C, Purdue

5. **Jacob Pullen,**
   G, Kansas State

CENTERS

JaJuan Johnson,
PURDUE

Johnson is the big man in the middle for a team returning loads of talent. He was good all year in 2009-10, but he really stepped it up in Purdue's three games in the NCAA Tournament.

OTHERS:

Adnan Hodzic,
LIPSCOMB

Vernon Macklin,
FLORIDA

Mike Tisdale,
ILLINOIS

Tisdale spent the offseason adding weight and strength to his 7–1 frame. He also got valuable experience by playing for a select team of college stars against the U.S. National Team.

THE RIVALRIES

YOUR FAVORITE COLLEGE basketball team might be a national powerhouse that packs thousands of fans into a huge arena. Or it could be a school near you that plays in front of a few hundred fans. But big or small, every school has one opposing team that its players gear up for more than any other. They all have one game that its fans look forward to all season long. That game is the big rivalry game. Some of this season's top college hoops rivalry games are long-standing traditions. Others have become big deals only recently. Let's check out a few of the very best!

WEIRD TRADITION

Several weeks before the game at Duke (at Cameron Indoor Stadium), students called "Cameron Crazies" pitch tents outside the arena to be sure they get into the game.

Duke VS. North Carolina

There aren't many things that fans of the Duke Blue Devils and North Carolina Tar Heels can agree upon, but there is this one: Their rivalry is the most intense in college basketball, and one of the most intense in all of sports.

Duke is located in Durham, North Carolina. The University of North Carolina is only about eight miles away in Chapel Hill. That stretch is part of what is known as "Tobacco Road" because the state produces so much tobacco.

One or the other of these schools—or both—usually is battling for the conference, or even the national, championship. The Blue Devils are the defending 2010 NCAA champions; the Tar Heels won it all the year before that. This year's battles should be just as fierce as usual!

Michigan State VS. Purdue

That's right—Purdue, not the University of Michigan. U of M is usually Michigan State's biggest rival. (Spartans' fans still await the days that their team plays the Wolverines— usually to get revenge for what Michigan's football team did to them in the fall!) Purdue's biggest rival has long been Indiana.

However, MSU Coach **Tom Izzo** has built his team into a basketball powerhouse, and any Big Ten team that wants to reach the top of the conference has to knock off the Spartans first. The biggest challenger to Michigan State's supremacy in 2010-11 appears to be Purdue, which makes this a rapidly growing rivalry.

WEIRD TRADITION

The Spartans made it to another Final Four last season. But the Boilermakers think that spot could have been theirs if not for a late-season injury to star **Robbie Hummel**.

WEIRD TRADITION

From 1959 to 1982, the schools did not play each other! Why not? **Adolph Rupp**, Kentucky's legendary coach for much of that time, hated Louisville too much!

STATE'S CHAMPS

These two schools have combined for nine NCAA championships. That includes seven for Kentucky (their first came way back in 1948 and won most most recently in 1998), and a pair of titles for Louisville (1980 and 1986).

Kentucky VS. Louisville

As the two biggest universities in Kentucky, the Kentucky Wildcats and the Louisville Cardinals battle for bragging rights in the Bluegrass State once a year. They only play in either Lexington (home of the Wildcats) or Louisville (home of the Cardinals). The 2011 game is in Louisville.

Adding fuel to this rivalry is **Rick Pitino**, who has been the Louisville coach since 2001. He was the coach at Kentucky from 1989 to 1997.

California VS. Stanford

This is a typical rivalry story: Two universities near each other, one a state school (California) and one private (Stanford). Both schools have great academic reputations, but are fierce rivals in athletics.

This one also features a coach who has switched allegiances. (To rivalry fans, that's like a Union soldier joining the Confederates—or vice versa.) He's Mike Montgomery, the coach of the California Golden Bears. Montgomery was the man who built the Stanford Cardinal into a solid NCAA Tournament team while coach from 1986 to 2004. But after a short stint in the pros, Montgomery returned to the college ranks in 2008 as coach of the Cardinal's biggest rival.

WEIRD TRADITION

One year, TV returned from a break to capture an on-court brawl. Stanford's Tree mascot and California's Oski the Bear were wrestling!

Akron VS. Kent State

Don't let the fact that these two schools are only considered "mid-majors" fool you: The rivalry between the Akron Zips and the Kent State Golden Flashes is as heated as any between big-time powers. And because the two schools are located only 14 miles apart in Ohio, they are plenty familiar with each other.

The schools have been playing basketball against each other since 1915. These days, they usually battle for the top spot in the Mid-American Conference.

WEIRD TRADITION

Rivalry or boxing match? Late in Kent State's victory over Akron in a game in 2008, a big on-court fight broke out. The next year, a Kent State player was ejected for throwing a punch— only 68 seconds into the game!

BYU VS. Utah

The Brigham Young University (BYU) Cougars and the Utah Utes traditionally are among the top teams in the Mountain West Conference.

Although Utah slumped last season after making the NCAA Tournament the year before, the two games between these schools take on extra significance in 2010-11 because Utah is moving to the Pac-10 (which will become the Pac-12) after that. That will mark the first time that the schools ever have played in different conferences.

WEIRD TRADITION
The rivalry is really important to the fans in the state of Utah (Brigham Young is located in Provo, while Utah is in Salt Lake City). Locals there call the annual football game between the two schools the "Holy War."

Georgetown VS. Syracuse

Georgetown and Syracuse became original members of the Big East Conference in 1979. Their rivalry has grown by leaps and bounds (or rebounds!) since then.

This rivalry is big, and it's not only because the two schools usually are pretty good and their games often affect the conference and national rankings. It's also because there have been so many great players and great games in the series. In the 1980s, they played each other eight times in the Big East tournament, including four times in the final game.

WEIRD TRADITION
Georgetown's coach is **John Thompson**. His dad, also John Thompson, became a villain in this rivalry when his Hoyas snapped the Orangemen's 57-game home winning streak in 1980. It was the last game ever played at Manley Field House. Thompson grabbed a microphone and taunted: "Manley Field House is officially closed!"

Kansas VS. Kansas State

Twenty-four home losses in a row to your most hated opponent will reduce the rivalry a bit. That's exactly what happened to the Kansas State Wildcats, who lost at home every which way—heartbreaking close games and lopsided blowouts—to the mighty Kansas Jayhawks every year for more than two decades.

But with an 84–75 victory in Manhattan, Kansas, in 2008, Kansas State ended the frustration, and the rivalry was back on. Now both of these schools are Final Four contenders.

WEIRD TRADITION

Before the big win in 2008, Kansas State fans saw the end of their agonizing home losing streak coming: They began entering the arena parking lots at 6 o'clock in the morning—13 hours before tipoff!

Texas VS. Texas A & M

Football is the biggest sport in this longtime rivalry. But the Lone Star Showdown also has included basketball since the teams first played on the court back in the 1916-17 season.

For a while, the Texas Longhorns' dominance quieted the basketball rivalry a bit. But now that Texas A & M is a force in basketball again—the Aggies are one of only two schools to win a game in the NCAA Tournament each of the last five seasons—the rivalry has been rekindled. It's so fierce, though, that the hoopsters might need helmets, too!

WEIRD TRADITION

How tough are these games? Texas coach **Leon Black** once told the *Fort Worth Star-Telegram*: "In my time as a player [1951-53], it was almost understood that there would be a fight in either the freshman game or the varsity game."

Dayton VS. Xavier

These two Ohio schools are located only about an hour's drive from each other. They are also both among the best in the Atlantic 10 Conference every year.

The Xavier Musketeers made it to the Sweet 16 of the NCAA Tournament last season, but the Dayton Flyers were the team that finished the season on a winning streak: They won the NIT Tournament.

WEIRD TRADITION

After a 71–58 win over the visiting Musketeers in 2009, several Flyers' players jumped onto a table on press row to salute their fans. That angered Xavier, which exacted revenge with a 76–59 win in the rematch in Cincinnati.

Pittsburgh VS. West Virginia

The name of this rivalry says it all: It's the "Backyard Brawl." The Pittsburgh Panthers and the West Virginia Mountaineers first played basketball in 1904, and they've played at least once each season since 1918-19.

When the Mountaineers joined the Big East in 1995, the schools became conference rivals, too. In recent seasons, both Pitt and West Virginia have been nationally ranked, making their games extra important.

WEIRD TRADITION

After his team's 82–77 victory in 1982, West Virginia coach **Gale Catlett** called Pittsburgh basketball "mediocre." That apparently got under the skin of Panthers coach **Roy Chipman**, who tacked the dig onto the bulletin board in the locker room—and left it there the remaining four years he ran the program.

WOMEN'S BASKETBALL

It's All About UConn!

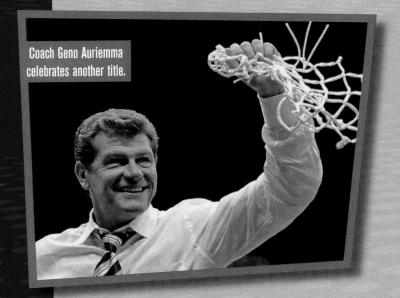
Coach Geno Auriemma celebrates another title.

THE NUMBER-ONE QUESTION in women's college basketball heading into this season is the same as the number-one question heading into last season: Can anybody beat Connecticut?

Last season, the answer was no. The Huskies, who went 39–0 en route to winning the national champion-ship in the spring of 2009, did it again in 2010. They were 39–0 for the second year in a row and won the national championship for the sixth time in the last 11 seasons.

Now, head coach **Geno Auriemma's** team enters the 2010-11 season riding a record 78-game winning streak. The Huskies are the favorites to win the national championship for the third consecutive season.

If they're going to go undefeated again this year, it won't come easy. They face a challenging schedule that includes nonconference games against national contenders Baylor, Duke, North Carolina, Stanford, and more, in addition to the usual slate of Big East games. "It's probably going to be our most difficult schedule ever," Auriemma says.

UConn faces that daunting schedule without center **Tina Charles**, the star player on last year's team. Charles averaged 18.2 points and 9.5 rebounds

Record Breakers

Before needing a second-half rally to beat Stanford 53–47 in last season's NCAA title game, Connecticut hadn't even come close to losing in its 78-game winning streak. The Huskies' first 77 wins in the string all were by at least 10 points.

Connecticut enters the 2010-11 season 11 games short of breaking the longest winning streak in NCAA Division I basketball history: the 88 consecutive games won by the UCLA Bruins' men's basketball team from 1971 to 1974. The longest women's college streak at any level is 81 games, by Washington University from 1998 to 2001. Here are the longest women's NCAA Division I strings:

78	Connecticut	2008-10
70	Connecticut	2001-03
54	Louisiana Tech	1980-82
46	Tennessee	1997-98
40	Texas	1985-87

UConn's 2009-10 team: national champs!

per game as a senior last season before becoming the top overall pick of the 2010 WNBA Draft.

Don't feel too sorry for the Huskies, though. Returning star **Maya Moore** is a 6-foot forward who was the Wooden Award winner as the college player of the year for the 2008-09 season. A first-team All-America in 2009-10, she averaged 18.9 points per game last season and enters her senior year with a career average of 18.7 points per game. Moore is on the verge of supplanting Charles as the school's all-time leading scorer.

Auriemma's incoming freshman class is loaded, too, with the likes of center **Stefanie** **Dolson** and guard **Bria Hartley**. Both of them played for the Under-18 U.S. National Team in the summer, and both of them figure to play key roles in their first college season.

In May, the Huskies visited the White House.

Who's Next?

CONNECTICUT'S Tina Charles won the Wooden Award and the Naismith Award as the best women's college player for the 2009-10 season. Charles has since moved on to the WNBA, though. (She's with the Connecticut Sun.) Her former teammate, **Maya Moore**, is one candidate for Player of the Year in 2010-11. Here are three other players who could take top honors in the women's college game.

Maya Moore

Brittney Griner

1. Brittney Griner
F, Baylor

She is coming off an amazing freshman season in which she averaged 18.4 points and 8.5 rebounds per game, set a women's record for blocks in a season, and helped carry her team to the Final Four.

2. Nneka Ogwumike
F, Stanford

She scored a career-high 38 points in a Final Four victory over Oklahoma last season that put the Cardinal in the national-title game against UConn. (The Huskies had to rally in the second half to win.) This year, her younger sister Chiney joins her at Stanford.

3. Ta'Shia Phillips
C, Xavier

The Musketeers actually boast two great players up front in Phillips and forward Amber Harris. Phillips was the Atlantic 10 Defensive Player of the Year last season and is a force on offense, too. That's a winning combination!

Angie Bjorklund

Talented Trio

DON'T HAND OVER this season's championship to Connecticut just yet. Several teams that were pretty good in 2009-10 could come back really strong again this year, including the likes of Stanford and Xavier. These three teams, though, have the best chance at stopping the Huskies' run to three straight titles.

1. Tennessee

The Lady Vols were the last team before UConn to win the women's national title. Guard-forward **Angie Bjorklund** headlines a strong cast of returning players that wants to avenge an upset loss to Baylor in last season's NCAA Tournament.

2. Duke

The Blue Devils were on their way to the Final Four last year before failing to hold an eight-point lead late in the second half against Baylor in the region finals. Still, returning stars **Jasmine Thomas**, **Krystal Thomas**, and **Karima Christmas** are joined by a great recruiting class.

3. Baylor

Though the Bears lost by 20 points to UConn in last season's national semifinal game (after their upsets of Tennessee and Duke), their roster featured five freshmen and had only one senior.

The Champions

Connecticut's championship last season was its sixth since the 2000 season, and its seventh overall. Here's the complete list since the first NCAA Women's Tournament in 1982:

Year	Champion	Year	Champion	Year	Champion
2011	_____	2001	Notre Dame	1991	Tennessee
2010	Connecticut	2000	Connecticut	1990	Stanford
2009	Connecticut	1999	Purdue	1989	Tennessee
2008	Tennessee	1998	Tennessee	1988	Louisiana Tech
2007	Tennessee	1997	Tennessee	1987	Tennessee
2006	Maryland	1996	Tennessee	1986	Texas
2005	Baylor	1995	Connecticut	1985	Old Dominion
2004	Connecticut	1994	North Carolina	1984	USC
2003	Connecticut	1993	Texas Tech	1983	USC
2002	Connecticut	1992	Stanford	1982	Louisiana Tech

COLLEGE BASKETBALL FUN

Find the Top 20!

Look through this basketball-shaped word grid and find the top 20 hoops schools (for men's college teams, that is). You can find them up and down, backwards, and even diagonally! Good luck! (PS: Don't look for the numbers, just for the school names.)

1 Purdue
2 Duke
3 Kansas State
4 Florida
5 Villanova

6 Michigan State
7 Ohio State
8 Gonzaga
9 Pittsburgh
10 North Carolina

11 Butler
12 Baylor
13 Washington
14 Kansas
15 Syracuse

16 Kentucky
17 Illinois
18 San Diego State
19 Missouri
20 BYU

```
                    V G Y
                  K M S B J Z D S Y
                E N Y Y O F I O Z O Y Q D
              W W Y M R P Y Z R L F G E Q R R D
            R B N P A X T D J U Y K E U K I U K H
          V X K X C N S M H K O V B X P F W G V E B
          E O I U F F E T A T S N A G I H C I M U U
          Z U M S L B B R X Y X S N D P K Y P I M U T T
          W L E Z Y U O Q Z G Q I B F J K Y H N A V L X
          L V A P L B N T M B U C M K E W Q E V R L Z E J F
          C N N T T F L U P M Y A G A Z N O G U P I F R E H
          Q S I O N I L L I T P X E M K Z P E P Q W B P T X
          B I D L G E Z Z Z U V H J W A S H I N G T O N I A V L
          Y O X O Y Y I A N R B Y Y R J D X A C M B T D J T D T
          U O N R M X M E V I L L A N O V A G S B M K B A S E H
          S V A K O K C I D S H G R U B S T T I P O S Y O R
          E M C V U P U X A U Z P I C U E V R M L H P C I X
          C A H R N K B S V M K E N T U C K Y O B I O T H F
          G T T N Q N J A E U E X I S O M R O L I Y V O
          O R T T A T E U X I E D T H E A X S E Y X Q I
          O X K F S D M U U Z N Q B D D Y I Z G A G
          N Z Z G R K A N S A S S T A T E J X R T B
          C H U Z R Y L B A K X P S K W L Y J G
          P T F E T A T S O G E I D N A S E
          A D I R O L F T E T J P K
          J T A W X P C X N
          K A R
```

To the Hoop!

Oklahoma star Danielle Robinson is off to the races! Or should we say, the hoop. Can you help her find the right path to get two points for the Sooners? Follow them carefully through the twists and turns!

A

B

C

Scoreboard Scramble!

When the scorekeeper got to the arena tonight, he found a big problem in his computer. All the important words he would need to report the game were mixed up. Can you unscramble these basketball terms? Then take the circled words and use them to find out the secret hoop slang at the bottom.

SSSTIA   __ __ __ __ (○)__

REFE OHWRT   __ __ __ __   __ __ (○)__

ILFED ALOG   __ __ (○)__ __   __ __ __

TSLEA   __ __ (○)__ __

OEUNDRB   (○)__ __ __ __ __ __

ULOF   __ __ __ __

KBOLC   __ __ __ (○)(○)

ERHTE INPOT   (○)(○)__ __ __   __ __ __ __ __

Secret slang: "__ __   __ __ __   __ __ __ __ !"

HAIL TO THE CHAMPS!

Now that you've read through this guide and gotten to know the college basketball teams for this season, it's time to make your pick: What team do you think will win the men's NCAA Tournament in the spring of 2011? (You can tell by our rankings what team is our pick to go all the way!) And while you're at it, check out the all-time list of Division I national champs.

2011 _____	1986 Louisville	1961 Cincinnati
2010 Duke	1985 Villanova	1960 Ohio State
2009 North Carolina	1984 Georgetown	1959 California
2008 Kansas	1983 North Carolina State	1958 Kentucky
2007 Florida	1982 North Carolina	1957 North Carolina
2006 Florida	1981 Indiana	1956 San Francisco
2005 North Carolina	1980 Louisville	1955 San Francisco
2004 Connecticut	1979 Michigan State	1954 La Salle
2003 Syracuse	1978 Kentucky	1953 Indiana
2002 Maryland	1977 Marquette	1952 Kansas
2001 Duke	1976 Indiana	1951 Kentucky
2000 Michigan State	1975 UCLA	1950 City College of New York
1999 Connecticut	1974 North Carolina State	
1998 Kentucky	1973 UCLA	1949 Kentucky
1997 Arizona	1972 UCLA	1948 Kentucky
1996 Kentucky	1971 UCLA	1947 Holy Cross
1995 UCLA	1970 UCLA	1946 Oklahoma A & M
1994 Arkansas	1969 UCLA	1945 Oklahoma A & M
1993 North Carolina	1968 UCLA	1944 Utah
1992 Duke	1967 UCLA	1943 Wyoming
1991 Duke	1966 Texas Western	1942 Stanford
1990 UNLV	1965 UCLA	1941 Wisconsin
1989 Michigan	1964 UCLA	1940 Indiana
1988 Kansas	1963 Loyola (Illinois)	1939 Oregon
1987 Indiana	1962 Cincinnati	